Making It Simple

The American Poetry Series

Volume 1—*Radiation*, Sandra McPherson

Volume 2—*Boxcars*, David Young

Volume 3—*Time*, Al Lee

Volume 4—*The Breathers*, James Reiss

Volume 5—*The House on Marshland*, Louise Glück

Volume 6—*Making It Simple*, David McElroy

David McElroy

Making It Simple

 The Ecco Press 1975

First published in 1975 by The Ecco Press
1 West 30 Street, New York, N.Y. 10001
Published simultaneously in Canada by
The Macmillan Company of Canada Limited
Printed in U.S.A.

The Ecco Press logo is by Ahmed Yacoubi.
Designed by Ronald Gordon.
The publication of this book is partially supported by
a grant from The National Endowment for the Arts.

Library of Congress Cataloging in Publication Data
McElroy, David.
    Making it simple.
    (The American poetry series; v. 6)
    Poems.
    I. Title.
PS3563.A2926M3   811'.5'4   75-14420
ISBN 0-912-94620-2

11/1975
Am. Lit.

PS
3563
A2926
M3

For Colleen

Acknowledgments:

ANTAEUS: *Dragging in Winter, Your Great, Great . . . , Nooksak Reservation, Report from the Correspondent They Fired, One For Your Hills and Sea,* and *McElroy, David F.*

CHOICE: *Legacy, The Valley of the Jolly Green Giant, Making it Simple,* and *Mean Mother Metaphor.*

EL IMPARCIAL: *Posada in Panajachel at Christmas,* and *Report from the Correspondent They Fired* (in both cases the poems were in translation).

GULFSTREAM: *Chichi Market.*

JEOPARDY: *Dream in Winter,* and *Posada in Panajachel at Christmas.*

THE MASSACHUSETTS REVIEW: *In Memory of Arden Davis, The Day After,* and *Up the Alcan.*

THE NATION: *Spawning in Northern Minnesota.*

SAGE: *Geology Field Trip.*

Anthologies:

THE AMERICAN POETRY ANTHOLOGY: *Dragging in Winter, Report from the Correspondent They Fired, Spawning in Minnesota, Making it Simple,* and *Ode to a Dead Dodge.*

INTRO #3: *Haunting the Matchless Mine Shack with Old Man Tabor's Ghost;* INTRO # 4: *Rebuttal to the Mild* and *Barbara's Cannery Ritual.*

Contents

I. Spawnings

Spawning in Northern Minnesota / 3
Your Great Great . . . / 4
Valley of the Jolly Green Giant / 6
Cache Bay: A Chippewa Girl's Open Grave / 8
The Earth Knows / 10
Legacy / 12

II. In Midstream, Baffled, Going Somewhere

One for Your Hills and Sea / 17
McElroy, David F. / 19
Girl Friday / 21
Up the Alcan / 23
In Memory of Arden Davis: Smokejumper 1966 / 25
Dream in Winter / 26
Molt of the Winter Soul / 28
Haunting the Matchless Mine Shack with Old Man Tabor's
    Ghost / 30

III. Whiter Waters

Three Bars and One Exit for Concrete, Washington / 35
Ode to a Dead Dodge / 39
The Day After / 40
South for the Winter / 42

Posada in Panajachel at Christmas / 43
Chichi Market / 45
Report from the Correspondent They Fired / 48
State of Siege / 50
Résumé on Whiteness / 51

IV. Approaching Some Ocean

Dragging in Winter / 59
Nooksak Reservation / 61
Where It Happens, When It Happens / 63
Puget Loons and Figure in Coat / 65
Rebuttal to the Mild / 67
Blue Song / 68
Barbara's Cannery Ritual / 70
Mean Mother Metaphor / 73
Ethiopian in the Fuel Supply / 75
Making It Simple / 76

Making It Simple

I   Spawnings

Spawning in Northern Minnesota

Under cracking pieces of the moon, eelpout
slap their milky bellies home. Water
breaking north turns granite at the mouth.
But here they batter, twist, and squirm over
and over each other, whipping dorsal fins
in a spinning roll, knocking flanks in the wake
of rocks—the splintered river dizzy with oxygen.

Birch explodes at thirty below, and spit
will scrape and clatter on the bank. Liquid fish
don't play games on a shallow bar.
In the bed and mix of the riffle, gills rake
water for air. Females plant gravel
with clouds. Flocks of males boil in a kiss
and make a hundred million chances work.

Cousin to codfish, an eelpout's liver
can't shrink goiters, but crossing moose
are sometimes whales, and any random otter
is a shark. Spawn floats the tinkling moon
downhill to a glacier's melted thumb
where limestone fossils crawl. Granite is ice.
The Mesabi is young, my county an ocean.

Your Great Great . . .

North by northwest of chimney smoke
and Ol Kaintuck my folks roped
me to an altar to burn the black
out of my bones. Electrodes shot
blue-Calvin volts from soul to cock.

My head spun with sparks.
My cowlicks whirled away.
The ropes broke. The bad black
inside squirmed out as chest hair.
I rose up, a scarred monster.

I saw God with hands on her hips
show me what to do when storms
charm my hunger. Stiff and stubborn,
no bears near, the redskins fixed,
I kissed a sinner when I was six.

"Your great great great great
granddad was Dan'l Boone," my dad
chanted, rubbing hands in sheep blood.
"Four greats is very very good,"
I chuckled, "but oh sometimes I'm mean
with the good that's mine."

Beware the smell of blood and onion.
Your Saxon past on red alert
will track you in the streets. Time
is out of synch. The west is won,
and I must eat the afterbirth.

I climb white buildings and throw
the airplanes down. She screams on top.
Despite your prayers, her torn dress,
you love this. Calmly, I kill, I eat up
the blonde babe we're supposed to save, then mate.

Valley of the Jolly Green Giant

Grass bones and buffalo chips
four feet thick
hatch Chinks and half-breed maize
stuck in a Swede's field. Cribs
disprove parity; REA makes
light in bulbs, love in grooves.

No red tendons crouch at dawn
on lunging thunder.
Love is a driveway horn
bumping soft as a barrow's belly.
Who hears bacon beller
when Daddy yawns at Guernsey tits?

Rare steaks roam the ramps.
Feeder-fed beef
hooked by the hock to a track slide,
subdivide, to U.S. Choice.
"For dining delight, come, relax in The Flame"—
the defecating buffalo you eat

and thirty-some Sioux in Mankato hanging
lax in crapped pants.
(That never happened in France.)
Wives bored by chores, who stared,
starved for a show, left red.
Pay as you go. Arrows point where.

In Minneapolis on Hennepin the cribs
of Gitche Manitou
store sheaves that Salvation's horn
dumps in. Mind gone green
down wrong turns, Hiawatha
begs Jim Crow for a shot of corn.

Cache Bay: A Chippewa Girl's Open Grave

Between my voice ratchets crank
the last logs home. Gasoline
fumes converge on the river bank,
and night comes rattling.

I fumble pockets, start to hone
my knife, but sit and stare
at that zygomatic arch, frontal bone,
a black patch of hair,

and shrunk skin caught in a knuckle.
Dangerous weather of pines,
a sulking ghost in the pelvic cradle
is smothered with a drift of pins.

Baby swimming down a river,
little rabbit legs,
little driftwood legs. A flivver
coughs in the wind and lags

on back to this scenic lumber town.
I test the second spare
blade with my thumb and know I own
the vertigo that's printed there.

A speed boat mutilates the moon.
"Night rain," prophesies
a laughing loon. Her lover was a loon—
his tarsal shanks were knives.

The outrage and sweat of stoking coal
on an ore boat west
of Keenaw Point made his soul
run red from the wrist.

She skipped school a week or better
then died of smallpox
without her grades. The fuss her brother
went to to make the box,

how he jewed with Dad and said thanks
(supper was ready by this time)
then drove off with the six cedar planks
whipping in binder twine.

Here he prayed, or whatever, maybe
sang something Indian
to her skull, then left and let the easy
seasons wander in.

The Earth Knows

George can't dance, won't drink, smoke,
say shit or take god's name in
vain. Starch belly, pasty face, poor.
Nothing's too good for cows and feet—
wine and olive oil in a bucket
cures hoof-rot in man or beast.

Nothing left to love but tired hills
eroded to a Sunday red. Driving tractor
gets him hard. I know that fever.
At fall plowing, the earth turning
like a Dublin whore rolling her scars over.

Seeds don't sprout on brow sweat alone,
he says. With heaven's own cow manure
and the special Israeli worms he plants,
his country bitch puts out manna
for twenty knock-kneed cows not worth
their weight in meat or milk.

A wise time to whittle his bones.
Just what he needs: a radio
to grow old with, flexible Bible
on his plate, soup cans to support him,
and a rooster to pray for.
The three kids married wrong.
The first with a shotgun,
the third with a Black,
and the gentle one with a railroad.

One day the milkman will drag
a smiling stiff from another manger
in Wisconsin, silage in the earhole,
the coat wet-warm like a new calf's hide
from a calm cow's drooling on it.

Work it right, and the earth knows,
he used to say. Like that spring he came
running yelling hallelujah leaping
the fences and furrows—my father,
blazing in the rain,
waving his cap filled with worms.

Legacy

You want straight hocks like Serina here.
See, the bag slopes up smooth in back,
round there; milk veins big;
pin bones wide for the calf;
no humpbacks, and watch for grubs;
wither clean, not wing-shouldered
from concrete floors all day.

He starts back there with money
and manure and ends at the head
with hay, grain, just outlay.
His prime four are: built-up black earth,
heat of the milk in his knees, cough
and suck of hungry titcups,
and chips from the trough that shatter like quartz.

When I was eight and we had sheep and the stove went out,
he hugged my headache hard in the light from the barn.
Hunkered in the dark, I scratched for broken
snow-fence slats—a dog eating lamb.
The broom thrown like a spear made blood
grease my hair. Buttons dug my ear
while we cried for all mistakes.

He strips hind tits for what a device
of steel can't guess and lectures on form.
I think how skaters cutting eights
lean and twist to fatten a track,
though I know she loves the logic of his hands.
When he makes her mine and things are final,
I'll chop elemental tears not to let her know.

II   In Midstream, Baffled, Going Somewhere

One for Your Hills and Sea

Animals collapsing in winter,
beautiful women in their attitude of crawling
over, and certain kinds of weather
dissolving in a minute, all swirl and mix
to the brown paste my brain is.

We will be slow to call this wisdom:
the third shepherd talking to zero,
the messenger who brought us forty-one
kinds of failure last year still surviving,
Tornado Frank pivoting over Kansas
on its cock, the weather in Qomox,
the writer who makes happen
as little as possible, the clouds
compared to crumbs on blue china,
and you, with no more hallelujah
than a glass of juice, not noticing
me not saying anymore I love you.

We are learning what to expect
from the state of paste my brain is in.
So many animals collapsing in women,
beautiful weather in its attitude of crawling
over, and certain kinds of winter

dissolving in a minute. And something
new now from nowhere,
a musical hero who sings to you:
The hills are like your this;
the sea is like your that.

McElroy, David F.

The altostratus barely oranges
over. Afternoon smog hollows
out its pumpkin pulp around me,
one sad seed. The sky
no longer with us, all streets
clean and equal—whatever
is found is fastened down.
I woke up thinking of my name card.

If I can dream, it's a free matinee
that delves into a pony's walking
with its patches through section B
of the oval, empty
municipal stadium.
Outside, the ginkgo trees
without sound in an old way
make love in no time at all.

Saturday's thin is Sunday's fat.
Now brandy pours in like direct-
distance dialing. My dog was good
for times like this. His nose
was snotty. He ate what I did
and couldn't swim either.

Somewhere they're playing jazz,
and you're blowing on the problem
that jams in back of a bad sax.
Some riffs make you Mama Amazon.
Drums explain your action
in the back as man goes down
in a wet burn, his fat on fire.
Or, you're just out from church
standing on a lawn with four chairs
eating jello because you've got red on.

The melody I'm thinking is my name card.
Do Re Me. My time on my hands,
I fingerprint the neighborhood red.
In the city's center, office of records,
in a metal rectangular file, alphabetically
bedded down, my name card
dreams up a horse with a blue butt,
while squeezed up tight and punched
to perfection is McEvoy, Gertrude R.'s card.

Girl Friday

Call a cactus Claudius (the typist
is Friday) and his affairs her escape
to ease another coffee break.
She combs her hair in a backless mirror.
You're part-time. You just work here.

Her paycheck is monthly, but his thirst
comes twice. Crisp and defended in a girdle,
every first and fifteenth the girl
will lean with a handful of rain
to the teapot desert on the windowsill.

Elena's typewriter points north
up the Rattlesnake. Her fingers run
the keys in spurts like plovers
hunting gravel. Squaw Mountain
is west, an index above the smog.

Right of her margin Hellgate Canyon
insults the town with a high-toned wind
from somewhere east of surplus wheat.
Say one thigh's a walleye, the other a loon,
and that scarf is really a trail of foam—

you'll worry the wrinkled plant hooking her hand.
Her brain has wrinkles, except the center
which is smooth but clearly demanding water.
North is a way of mind, and she can't fool
the north nor the push and pull of the poles.

The window protects her from pigeons and April
and, last year, the single swan,
while veins that rinse her brain skid
down an open throat and run
for cover of her dress on a wilderness of skin.

Up the Alcan

So ends the story of The Boy
And His Flying Machine And Dog.
I throw the book on the dash
and keep driving the pickup
in low gear, twenty miles an hour,
my throw-out-bearing shot,
a hundred miles to the next gyp
joint across the Yukon.

Sancho Panza, wonder dog,
drools on my thigh. Fat, dumb
and happy in the golden dream
of the Great Pika Rabbit Corral.
His chubby toes quiver in pursuit.
He moans wisely then yawns.
The mouth that ate the west.

I open Sister Mary Gilbert's
book across the horn
on the wheel. On the one hand
I steer. On the other, I push
the words flat against the page
so they won't bounce off
across the tundra with the bears.
This poem's about the undertow.

This road was built for war.
Curves, loops and doodles
on a flat plateau made convoys
safer from strafing that never
happened here. The chrome ram
on the hood sweeps the horizon
in a steep turn. I'm a hero
on the prowl.

Without warning the road
coils in a pile behind a tree.
Caught in the vortex,
both hands on the wheel,
the words fall down, break,
and the page comes tumbling after.
A coyote whips by.
One quick look:
the zeros in his eyes.

In Memory of Arden Davis: Smokejumper 1966

The spotter slaps our legs and we tumble
from the Doug down to sudden silence.
Bad form, the plane and then the ground
spin above me. Behind me, Arden leaves
like a fetus, perfect, a white boulder
heading home through the green air.

For a moment our bodies are all we have,
nervous circuits in space. Static lines
snap. Our chutes explode out round.
In shrouds we swing just right and dream our lives.

Eskimos stare at the same nightmare each March—
that perfect approaching peeled orange.

We fall and turn like clockwork
over tundra, trees, avoiding the Tanana
going back on itself in sine curves
S-ing to the sea with a current so certain
even geese go down. Below,
good men are stumps, bad for the ankles.

I yell at my friend. We wave our arms
like angels. We've decided. We're staying.

Dream in Winter

for Jim Welch

One eye spinning down the rifle
and the other tracking heat makes less
and less difference: dawn, pink timber,
a gorge, at last the bull elk running—recoil
and blast. My visions collide on meat.

Flatten the map in your head, reverse
the land. Here my poky road curves
on versions of your work, the lizard in my brain.
All rest rooms are clean on Highway 2,
and we use English for food; hands are for asking.

Women call us cold. Those that help us
talk are gone or Indian. April in Pete's Ravine,
the blind one rode a sorrel and sang on pitch,
"O mint, mica, and wintergreen." When you're drunk
the fat man calls you chief.

That time we drank the last wine
your hometown stuck in your throat:
Blackfeet flint is tactile, men talk
in a ring, their hands talk too,
songs for meat veer over a woman's hair.

When the star that is a hunter with a packsack
comes up, I'll dream. No words, driving west
in winter, my sight fans out like a hand to the next
warm thing moving. You're waiting with a pack.
I zero to your gesture in flat country.

Molt of the Winter Soul

A warm noisy family adopted me
from the mileage I used to make,
from silences I thought of
as stunted spruce standing in groups
on moonscapes along the Alcan.
Just night and more winter coming
to track the whiff of my exhaust.

I thought I'd made it.
I went south, doubled back
in snow, walked backward
in snow, dissolved my trail
south again through water.
In soft shoes I lost my smell
in Seattle and New York, New York.
It didn't work.

I've changed my skin almost,
the orphan crust sloughing off
to show a darker warmer layer.
Again tonight it is early winter
in the temperate zone of America.
My wife and children are fast asleep
in blackness, breathing easy.

My hand scratches pages in hunger,
a patchy pinto creature pawing
old snow down by the willows.
A twig snaps in the hall.
From the darkness of my son's room,
the cat studies my movements
for hours. Her frozen gold-slits,
the quiet eyes of the arctic lynx.

Haunting the Matchless
Mine Shack with
Old Man Tabor's Ghost

Baby Doe's shack she died in
can't hold heat. Even light
from kerosene (you can still smell it)
shivers through tapered shakes to spatter
silver on slag the pump douched out.

Weather enters slow: at the collar
when your head is turned, molasses oozing
down your back. Or the single cone a chipmunk
stripped in the washpan. Cold fronts bulge
the plastic windows in. Beyond coiled
cable, pulleys, ore cars, and the ore chute,
the Matchless shaft sleeps with no weather,
a coin slot waiting for the moon.

Legends say you sleep here, rolled up
in the shape of your clothes ironed flat
and folded for packing. Your ventilated
two-tone shoes hang by the heels, breathe
of an easy life on a tropic trip.
Baby Doe, your other woman, left staring alone
for years after, left nothing—sticks
for kindling in the corner, a strand
of hair in a saucer. She might have been

a tanager in from sleet and sun. Hunger,
your will and last words wiped her out.

You barge in some nights, as I just did,
a damn good ghost or jug in the wind
and wake with cold your pretty Baby Doe.
The door ajar banging a chair like the rudder
of a scuttled bomber. No rhythm to the wind.
She sits up, sings insane for meat and greens,
wraps her feet in burlap, runs to town
for food and humans, while a cross fox follows
through the willows, in his jaws a china cup.

My boots hit hollow on piss pine cull
laid diagonal but springy with weight.
Shadows mimic us gothic to the wall.
We pump our shoulders for the right effect:
me the comic, you the heavy
out of synch, an old movie to laugh at.
This kitty-corner floor makes north
all wrong on a bad night and the car stalled.
A trap door might drop us down
to hidden spuds. Would I weigh the same
in Chile? The Senate made you fat.

Millions in silver made you wise.
You got elected. You bought your bust.
The old story, silver crashed with you broke,
no wiser, the sad ending. A convenient cold
in Denver left you gasping with a private
face. Through wavy windows you saw
the pink sunset collapsing like your lungs.

Legends say you sleep. I say you trap
mice for steaks, eat ants, eat your hands
and cock, supple as smoke in empty rooms.
Fat dancer with light feet, hollow handles,
your food shows through like lesions
on my X-rays, or the frozen bugs on this moonlit
screen that frames a timbered ridge
and river's fork. You mine the moon
for cobalt, blue with cold, no wood,
no weather. Meanwhile back in a funny flick
where all gestures slant one way, lovers die
like this shack. First a jerky bird flies out,
then the light goes out and then the heat.

III   Whiter Waters

Three Bars and One Exit for Concrete, Washington

No bingo in Concrete!
reads the bald scrawl on the door
where Fellows of the Eagle
chug beer and talk logs,
the last elk nailed, steel-
heading, anything hot.
Black nigger in white pants
is a sign of rain.
Ever see one in a pickup?

Women go the color of stone
from years of walking on.
The last dream of love split
when slacked-off chokers broke
a chaser's tin hat and head
up Crevice Creek in '60.
The whistle punk packed
him out in a crummy.

No movies, music, lipstick.
What Catholics there are
have little voice and now,

no bingo, less vice.
They play the Tarheel Stomp
at the Castle. That's thirty miles
to dance with pussy in Woolley.

2

Next door is the store
of Carmardella, and ten
steps more is Carmardella's.
The front's a joint,
the back's a bar.
Mandolin, velvet bullfight,
real garlic—Latin in the back.

He drinks like Mitchum
in a T-shirt at his bar,
orders beer from daughters
that don't date. (One plain,
one pasta coming up
in this world.) O Sole Mio
sits tight in the Wurlitzer.
Cosa Nostra could care.

3

The Hub is where it's at
for bottled or tap, sporting
goods, gloves, beer nuts,
and boots. Men talk logs,

or be cool like Strand,
age 58, who waxed
the town clown's ass, broke
his badge, jaw, and sternum
for messing with his daughter,
not a day over desperate.

Time goes if Fred is there
or you can shoot pool.
The only place in town
where Walter the only Black
could buy beer period
and later with a cagey
game win it back
in 1971.

4
Main Drag out of town zig-
zags through an old pain and exits
like suspended shadows of my hometown's
one straight street collapsing like pipe
on the great plowed plains.

I grew up like this, a dull plant
in the morning of the stiff hand
cramped from shit forks and cow tits.
My childhood snapped in a twist
of chaw, dissolved in the dribble
on the chin. I ran away at ten.

Eat shit, my people. I left
and you're embarrassed into rage.
Your town's insane but dying right.
The headstone's there. A concrete
plant shutdown, biggest thing around.
The only noise, trucks and rain.

Good-bye to the men who are men
and the bucks they shoot
and the people they did.
Good-bye to nervous women
and their curtains,
to the town team that better win,
to Lady's Day on the 4th.
Good-bye to the third armpit
of the world.

I pass through now, exit,
head for home and a better scene
as one by one the minutes
bloom open to a warmer dark.

Ode to a Dead Dodge

Now corn pushes past the foam-
rubber front seat where it sprouted,
pale and aiming like a drunk for the light
up front where glass and guessing
became concrete. One ear taps
code on a dud horn.

The corn drives on, gunning till fall
the engine, which, as it now stands,
is a sumac, V crotch in the stem,
four-barreled leaves doing the job
while all around hang those red fuzzy
berries. Very good, I've heard, for tea.

The Day After

I step off the bus into heat
the stink bug knows
tunneling through cantaloupes
rotting by the road.

A sticky yellow world slowly
rolls me along the strange streets
I usually piss in in dreams
after some dynamic good-bye.

No kids or toys to trip on now.
Uncut shrubs shag out
over the walks. Doors are open
as if to ask, Are you a breeze?

In one, a singer tears his heart out
in the walnut TV console.
The man watching, smokes
quietly in a wheelchair.

In another an old couple plays cards.
He in shorts, she in bra and panties,
they play with their veins
and stretch marks showing.

Finally, a place with a vacancy
for me and a rucksack to fill.
No pets, excessive drinking, or parties,
the landlord says. No problem,

I say, thinking of the wife, dog,
beer, and head I had.

South for the Winter

That burdock, lamb's-quarters and foxtail
will join spoiled silage and milk
gone hard starch in the hybrid ear,
perhaps to ride the wild silo
in a pigeon's coo, or sleep the hollow
basswood out on a raccoon's back.
Hunters will organize this eighty for a bag of two,
no luck in the neighbor's rows plucked of their organs.

This pumphouse and woodshed
can stand itinerant cats
who pitch and toss in the tumult of grass
and split night with the mix of their seed.
A beach is odd: a skinny field
fencing a flat, and goiters unheard of.
Harmless locusts, the plankton tick
in the give and take of the waves.

Point to Mérida from Hunt's silo
and you confront a twelve-hour day—
like Mayan pyramids, manure piles
are mostly chores waiting to flower.
Call your income to the stanchion.
Bless producers with an extra scoop.
Kick hay to the drooling bull, chained
for something some entry in his book might do.

Posada in Panajachel
at Christmas

Beat the turtle's belly, you friends
of Mary. Mary needs a bed. The lizard
in the leaves and I in the pines might learn

that wail and whacking though we parade no mouth
in that direction. Your tongue is not our mother.
No carols, whites here stuff money in the throat.

On *noche buena* firecrackers kick
the hills where rocks and cornstalks lean,
and the shell of the turtle rides a rocking hip.

A crèche rides six women out of step:
Mary and the manger, the ass and plaster cattle
(the straw is vinyl), Joseph wobbles in back.

Still no word. Women nurse their babies anyhow.
Their shawls are pregnant with bread and peppers,
and pubic bones are rubber in the heat.

Star on a stick, the moon half up, the shell
and echo of the turtle refine volcanos
though wind braids garlic in the smoke.

The tongue and song the lizard is
relates the leaf and night bug's arc
while men break down the last right door.

That plastic star with sixty sides,
candle, and an open top can't break
the turtle in the bay or coot's wedge at dawn.

Chichi Market

I look at light shinny half-
way down the lone tree
flaking bark in the square,
then jump like jokes through canvas
tarps not really shading
Mayan women who share
a good one on me
on Market Day usually
in Chichicastenango no less.

Avocados big as cantaloupes
for four cents are worth a laugh.
Prices here make broke gringos
rich and sheepish to the folks
selling fruit because it's what
they do. Local colors have equal
value. This quirky light
is into everything like the barrel
of monkeys routine. Agile
as air, it bounces around, picks up
each tomato, balancing, holds it
still, then licks the red off.

Searching for treasure,
one more white with a dollar,
I seem to slant when I stand.
I look at light and use
the squint I've used for snow,
one eye closed, the other nearly.
My face, monkey-funny
and ghostly old inside out,
a comic mask of what I've been.
In shirts I'm a medium.
In pants I'm 30 by 32.
In shoes I take heavy steps
with Cortes and Alvarado
clowning on my back.

The kids kill me, call me
Gringo, Gringo, *Yanqui!*
White shirts in white air,
they run away like caribou
to a slow ropey river
that ties a granny in the valley
where my people hung hundreds.

On the colonial cathedral steps
the farmers seriously swing
incense over candles and offerings
of corn on the cob for Mary,
mother of blood, and for Chac,
our rain god. When jokes are over
I'm just a man and what I carry

home to eat. A woman sits
cross-legged on the cobblestones
selling goods from her lap.
Her skirt sags between thighs
with shelled corn, the colorless corn
man's made from.

Report from the Correspondent They Fired

Juan, the moron next door,
dreams in green feelings.
The parrot perched on his head is real
friendly, and the avocado right
in his hand is a handful of green.
The brown hand molds its package
around the meat, and the meat molds
around the pit dead center
in the palm. When he is hungry
the avocado is good to eat.

The river standing by is not
a snake, neck bulged out
with bottled news of guerrillas
coming alive in the Guatemala
gloom upstream. The gun butt,
the splintered cheek piece bobbing by,
is only pine, a *campesino*'s table leg.
Water can't talk. The river
and the parrot know their place.
Barges stuck in mud are chunks
of chocolate good to eat.

Crazy with the heat, waiting for mail,
I try to read the river where it curves.
Even boatmen miss the point.
My neighbor and I swing out together
over the bank on a log swing hung
from a ceiba. The dumb bird clings
in Juan's hair turning off and on to green.

Today the butcher killed a sow
then hung a red flag out
to signal flies and mothers in.
Consuelo, another widow dressed up
in black, empty basket on her head,
comes down the road for jowls
and pork brains. The afternoon glows
caramel on her arm, beer-bottle smooth.
In her snappy black cat eyes, slivers
of light damn me, the company I keep,
and my mox-nix vegetarian politics.

Ah *vaya*!
Two strange ones swinging by the river,
we could be friends, we could be hams
curing in the shade, good to eat.

State of Siege

Nights in the hot country, toads
big around as LPs
lug their scuffing guts for food,
jumble around rings of light—
the white coast of the Mayan's eye
where fear climbs out
sticks its tongue out
at bugs making stars of themselves.

The skin, the bulgy scrotum
gravy skin of giant toads.
On their backs, the classic design,
comic mask, real warts.
Really the aging face of Cortes
pulsing in the street. Toads,
stomp one, and bugs
belch out both ends.

Résumé on Whiteness

I. Vital Statistics

"This morning, this evening, so soon."

My name got started in a car.
I had two choices: first a wall
then a door.
I turned white in the countdown.
They unloaded my mom before dawn.
I was born at four
at the start of a war,
the third child of the woodcutter,
the second son. Pain of passage,
the alien air,
my belly button sewed and foreskin cut—
I felt what millions feel
on that floor.
My back ached for a week.
Our heads assembled in lines like belts
of bullet blanks. Bracelets still
keep us straight.
My first vision was a light bulb,
the second, stainless steel.
The third, the target nipple.

II. Education

"Stop on over for some tea.
You'll get steak, potatoes and me."

Her face hung white in the hall,
folded long like a towel. She did all
the right things. She pinched my nose for farting
on Sunday, washed my face with spit
and wiped me white. She taped my toe
in summer, fluffed the pillow I spit at.
I slept on a catcher's mitt. I came to
at dawn, green and steaming as Father's fields.

That summer, Sister disappeared into the neighbors.
My brother goosed Audrey the cow in heat
up to the elbow. I stamped a kitten flat
and won a cigarette. Look, my hand is yellow,
twelve, and hollow. Hear it whistle to your migraine,
Mama? When you call me water boy and send me off,
the mason jar enlarges my hands. My face to the glass,
I run to a world that's weirder. Bullseye,
fisheye, the field coming at me, fences zooming up
and out. Then a dim man warping into red
on a red bailer. This water for Father,
so cool and clucking in the jostle.

A white sheet hung on the line to signal supper.
Mother prayed for rain, sang Sinatra
to the sink and checked her legs for purple.
I played Indian against my brother, never

losing with a squirt gun. Blue jeans and no color
kept me common. No fasting alone on a hill,
no visions but Audrey and the bull—we never
learned our water names. The week it rained
with the hay down green but the grain
in, we sat on sacks of seeds, sweated,
and beat our meat to manhood.

III. Experience

"Shine, Shine, save poor me."

Gray shirt and straight hair stamp me
like you want: a Roman with a good job,
and loose change for your beggar pitch.
The ugly stub from your little limb
that spoiled in the heat is worth a peso,
eight and a half cents American.
Mother said there would be days.
I'm white and burning in the plaza.

I tan orange and silly as the moon.
These freckles could be cheese or craters
but spots are rumored smallpox
along the coast. The simple cold
I carry could knock you out.
Among your flat handsome faces
and thick smiles my nose juts red
and runny like a sore thumb
commanding you to leave me be.
The quarter I drop in your coconut cup
is a happy pill. It'll let you down.
Eagle and Miss Liberty got the clap.

Heads or tails, I'm here to teach
you English or rectify your rivers—
the Usumacinta plumbed straight,
the Orinoco about its business.
The people you think I stand for
are serious about your sun, its beaches,
domestic service, bananas and oil.
Your numbers, they tell me, are growing
in our only frontier. The bucking bronco
on my belt buckle must tell you something:
disciples and conquistadores follow
dramatic symbols—bird, beast, or bitch,
a moving picture from the angel factory.

Yesterday I was on my way somewhere.
The letter from the embassy with commas
sown like oats through the English
said I was chosen and should hurry.
I only stopped to cool off in the town shower
and soap my sour hair when I saw the light.
These calico mountains flattened suddenly
away like a cat in the rear-view mirror.
I was sentenced in the glare
of a hundred kids. Then you with your beggar
self opened my car, crazy, your pet parrot
squawking on your shoulder, shitting
on your money maker. You said, All the dead
are white and walking backward.

I tried my best. Good afternoon, I said.
How are you called?
I am called David.
We were not converted and I gave you money.

Now at noon the second day, the light
so high slams down white. Bright birds
and men wash out. The plaza fountain
trickles from the brim in a broad sheen,
attracts a pale dog where a rainbow
warps light blue just above the mud.
Even your kinky hair and rich skin fade
into adobe and dust as you hobble off
to look for a tourist with better clothes
lost in a good town for sudden religion.
With north gone, where's my face?
There is little to say, less to hand down.
I'll keep my jazz in a jar in the fridge.

Last night I sneaked past the sleeping clerk
in the hotel out to touch dark earth,
feel fur, and swim naked in the river.
Turning to breathe new air, my elbow
rose up black and classic as your volcanos,
and my face ran away with the moon.

IV   Approaching Some Ocean

Dragging in Winter

Sometimes the sea lays
back nasty white like a girl
(get it?) when draggers anchor
down in weather. And let's say
the sky moved in furniture.
To pass the time, this swirl
of fog is a blanket thrown
over the seabed. What we want
swims in limbo by the tons
under the covers. We're bored
with the diesel's throb, nonchalant
with our handsome hard-ons.

We roll smokes and act
like men of the sea who fit
their own rugged beauty, acting
natural rolling smokes.
Ham it up. We're ugly, get it?
Money is looks when you're broke
in the hole with Friday beat
by next week. Even women break
down like jobs or weather,
cry and skunk you on the beach.
Our skipper jokes about winter
fogs when he-men fuck skate.

"What the hell with time to kill—
and the hole's a dead ringer."
Ugly for love, we imagine fishermen
who get it. The skate's wings, not fins,
smacking on the deck. The tail stinger
you chop off. Stuff a plaid shirt
in that shark-mouth or you'll get hurt
again. Lug your lover to a fo'c'sle
bunk, hook your fingers in gill
slits. Make the most of it, wish
on a star, jab your aching eggs
up the cold ancient fish flesh.

On land we'd act natural, pure
dirt from so much sea—the sea, dirt
cheap and flop-house mean. Who coiled
the kelp like bedsprings? Furniture
broken in a dirty mind? We've all called
that mermaid up, the prettiest flirt
in town who forgot her tail was a fin,
who just wanted someone human, weak
like Robert Young, the American father,
for staying lovely with, loving less
and less, bound in marriage back to back
like purebred dogs stuck together.

Love is ugly, and the child, born wet.

Nooksak Reservation

These homes have one story,
back shed, front porch,
a brief brown yard.

The river boils suckers in the rain.
The river sliding by—
all four sides are different.
Only the name stays around:
Nooksak.

Rain for a week and a half,
now sunlight gets a word in.
One story:
The Devil and His Wife.

Jimmy Jack stirs the dirt
with a red stick from a broken rose,
draws arrows to Plymouth
to river to Buick and back,
then pokes the toe of his right black boot.
The one place light shines.

No big scenes here.
The white clouds will take
their five-dollar tickets
and leave soon.

But here it is. It's over again,
the old story,
the old words
without motors
parked around the porch.

Where It Happens,
When It Happens

The butcher, the butler,
the bitch and the rat
don't blush and won't chatter
or move too much. They pose
for you, comfy in the color
they know you shoot them as.

Where you go, there you are.
You zoom us to the coup
and interview: Who and Why
on your mind. Subjects glance
this way, expecting to find me
crouching in the lens
like a bullet
wearing a blue suit.

The nonchalance goes on.
It's up to you to get the picture.

So what did she seem?—
the exotic Iowan last week,
wading up the beach as the green
sea slid from her licorice hips
and settled down
like underpants.

Your best technique makes her
misty (nude or not)
like posters for the poor:
a cream sky dished up for thunder,
the eyes up against the light,
speed high, and f-stop wide.

Caught for current events
in the last act of reaching out
for sand—she stood so close.
About 3 feet.

But the sky goes on
to land like jets in Kansas
after dark, and the rain
that really falls, falls calmly
with or without mercy
in patches from Elko to Boise.

And the stone fox, now a mother
with a towel, steps freely
through your framing to slap
her son for eating paper in public,
before dissolving beautifully
behind a bent white
who happens along
surrounded in a sousaphone.

Puget Loons
and Figure in Coat

Steep g's. Their wing tips flex concave
in tight turns where good scenes warp with weight.
They sight down on downtown smokestacks, smog,
log booms, bay, and you, the aphasic bum
on the trestle hunching home with oatmeal to the tunnel
you know but can't name. Cops call you Honest John
because you're old and jobs you pull are puny.

Light fingers, this bad weather keeps you clean.
Breaking wind, blaming spiders, you jabber
down the line becoming less. Barnstorm pilot,
the seat of your pants, baggy as a chimp's ass
in pants, still steers, and air is everywhere.
Two loons crisscross away so you see one.
The mate flies dead in parallax.

With passes east choked on snow, grain freights
stalled off schedule and barley seepage nil,
no chicken in the pot, no wonder water birds
are girls you rolled in Rio thirty years ago.
The gold gone, your last engagement flopped in Nome.
These tracks curve into the earth, vanish to a point
you're walking to, the next rock after crust.

Open barns and your wing walker passed away.
You can't fly for wages, nor dive for visions
in strong water the pulp plant makes, riding
a loon's back down, going on air your bones hold—
those Indian summers coalesced in the femur.
You lumber blind down runways of my blood.
If I blink you're off and gone light as lint.

Rebuttal to the Mild

I skipped school to hunt with Barry on his furlough.
The lake where we camped never showed a ripple
except the night we packed the goatmeat and hides
down off the slide. We washed the caked blood and sweat
from our hands and necks. We smiled and shivered with the lake.

The bugling of bulls in the canyon was thin as coyotes
in a sleeping-bag dream. We left the heads—
appropriate trophies for jays and ravens. His goat
broke a horn cartwheeling, dead. Mine, both horns
long ago, living. A hind leg had a jagged knit.

So when the good girl on the panel for peace implied
your copter was evil, I felt like hooky. No excuses,
our goats were billies and I'm still here, sick of you
and what the C.O.s make you, sick of blondes who make
our lives flat as English hills leveled with sheep.

In bed or bag I dream of coyotes and monsoons.
Cong girls lovely with guns drift from rock
to rock in my occupied dreams. In Belfast, too, my grand-
mother swung a stocking filled with rocks into a Catholic's
privates—beautiful, skillful, off her fat ass,
fighting for god, cussing and killing us Catholics.

Blue Song

Sixty percent of what you are
you got from me baby, you said
before you split in a red cutlass
convertible whaling away.

My Story: Part I
The Americanization of gray boy.
White friends wrote postcards.
What's it like, nigger-lover?
Black friends gave me family,
dropped off the lover part.

Part II
This now, you gone, me defrocked—
always knew it could happen,
left naked nearly, but acting Sippi,
argyle socks and gambler hat,
Georgia ham in one hand
and you bad hammer gone.

I read the paper.
In Sagwan, Alaska, an opening.
Wanted: man to watch hangar,
take weather, plow runway,
stay alive slowly, play radio.

The redneck leper inside me
forty percent
wise with no-exit understanding
chops his last leg off
with a nasal twang.

Certain speech lets us sing,
puts warm hands
on the world and a loud house
all around with a special queen
hundred percent
full rich in a blue song
full vowels and flashing gold
of O earrings.

I'm here doing right.
Me and the two babies
waiting for the phone
playing Hendrix, me smoking,
sick on wine, my feet
stuck up on the table
where you know it's cold
without our warm nigger love.

Barbara's Cannery Ritual

The belt goes by for days
lugging sockeye to our knives.
Dressed white and horny as a nurse,
I stand all day. One foot and then
the other. The belt goes by.

One fish plus four flat strokes
make two fillets. Meat in one tub,
guts in the other. A female, I stab
her head, flop her over. Four strokes
divide bone and guts from meat.
The eggs spurt pus-yellow.
Chuck them in the gut tub.

The belt splice goes click-click
on the rollers. Toward me, by me, away
down the line of working women, all white
except for green gloves, black boots, and me
their friend. I strop my blade keen.
The belt conveys my eyes to the window
and out a chute where green swells
come to relax on the sand for days.

We chatter over machinery. My neighbor
can't laugh and isn't half as fast.
Her smock hides an ass so flat

she had to stack two pillows
to get one kid. Our talk clicks
like marbles in a bag for days.

The belt goes by for days.
When I quit this shift some say good-by.
I disappear in the woodwork
of their town, but my hands remember
the knack of strokes when I butter bread.

Mac trucks are loading canned salmon
bound for Kansas and casseroles.
Forklifts shuttle in and out.
The drivers, acting smart as horses
frisking in the wind, pivot on the ramp
and slam crates down hard on the truck bed.
This Grade A meat won't show the net
bruise or pattern of the scales. Children
know white milk comes from a wax box.

Tomorrow's off. Tonight I'll do
my hair and bake a frozen pie.
I'll watch tv and plan parties where oildrums
bang with ice and beer, and clothes feel
so soft you fall asleep just wearing them.

The belt goes by.
We hose down soon.
The Tajlum was high boat
at Salmon Banks, the Tender said.
Tomorrow he's due in, running the late
tide out the Strait. He'll walk tired

up our hill, smelling of sea and diesel.
I'm in the kitchen boiling ferns
or out back bringing in the wash.

Last week I heard his fingers gallop
on the fender in the front yard a moment
before he caught me from behind
pulling panties off the damp line.

Mean Mother Metaphor

In the cold ocean only whales are warm, also walrus
in a foot of fat, and specks of birds on slate waves
bobbing in the chop.

Squid, skate, salmon, merman and maid, seaweed, all
dissolve deep in degrees of gray, wave coldly
and swim the same.

In radar light, currents click rocks through tons of oxygen
like the liquid popping of your spine. The Aleutian chain
erupts muffled

as the belch in a cow. Atomic testing beats the bony plates
of the sturgeon's head, vague as human data in my dreams
of news reports

watched alone in a blue room where I am usually smoking.
In the dumping ground cod search car seats. They signal coldly
and drive the same.

Perch stare out bus windows. The octopus fingers an ash tray.
Polyps grow on a radio, and a starfish eats a doorknob
tight as a fist.

I eat you when words don't open. Taking off your clothes
you grow blacker and fabulous, larger in the room
and in my eyes.

In my cold poems the white chemicals from your body
stick to my tongue, warm and bitter like a shiny penny
soaked in salt.

Later, I'm lucid but weaker and pumping gas for my own
    ambulance
before the wrecker dumps me and metal in the sea.
My splash ripples out

and in the tympanum of the killer whale sounding for the right
whale's tongue, a chunk of pulp behind baleen—sweet
as passenger pigeon.

Off Point Moler and Amchitka mad hulks breach for air,
erect and small in reported fog. The killer clings.
The tongue spurts blood

black with hemoglobin, and the right rolls fin out.

Ethiopian in the Fuel Supply

A spot of jungle fever
lipstick on your black forehead,
a silk sheet from Gramma's past
draped and sari-ed over you
to hide your 'fro,
ski-jump breasts,
and jungle-bunny highpockets,
a girl friend done up the same,
and a foreign accent
(too teeketts plees)
let you in to see the movies—
no-ass Lana actin uppity,
Cary Grant too noble
to score—on the clean side
of St. Louis. Ushered
down front and white center, you
(my future lover, wife)
passing survival,
rolled your shoulder,
popped your finger,
said, Girl,
tell me whad I say?

Making It Simple
December 8, 1969

Married for one year
plus a week and a half,
I watch my black wife, Colleen,
lean from the big chair
toward Vanessa, who is puzzled
in soft lamplight.

They are looking for answers
the abacus can give them.

The round wood beads
in ten rows of ten
are red
orange
yellow
green
and blue
repeated twice
counting down.

In the kitchen Kevin is ten,
but she is nine.
Adding is easy,
take-away is hard.

Mama says
you can subtract by adding.
With pencil and paper
she draws eight pudgy birds,
"How many more birds
do you need
to make twenty-five?"

The many fingers of my wife are lovely,
slender, like the eyes of her daughter
who now has arched her supple arms
back over her head
like the horns of the American gazelle.
She says, "I don't get it."

They are looking for answers
the abacus can give them.

They are looking for the pudgy birds
that won't come home.
The soft Oriental partridges
fluffed up against the cold,
stuffed with buds, roosting in the tops
of birch trees at twilight
when I was fifteen and counted
with a long brown gun.

The wood beads click softly
like jellybeans,
all flavors.
In buttery light

they look full and spongy
as enemy babies
stacked on a path
in ten rows of ten.
The red so real
it's phony blood.
The last rows,
by accident,
green and blue as produce.

Adding is easy,
take-away is hard

We are hungry for numbers:
correct, no or yes, but definite
like getting pregnant.
My wife bends down with answers
mean as wine that she can't give
Vanessa, for whom my love is legalized.
In some states the papers come soon.

Mother and daughter,
the yellow space between
defines exactly a gold goblet
or two faces in relief,
the profiles classic and blended
from Ife
Chinese
and Seminole.
A handsome hodgepodge, American
even.

When my wife steps out to me from the bath
her wicked limbs are lavish
and our secret, royal.
Our girl climbs from the tub,
eyes closed, feeling for a towel.
Her pussy is perfect without hair,
like the sweet blue clefted plums
waiting for us on the trees
at our first home this fall.
I hand her a towel and feel the power
of all our lost fathers.
I have tasted my sperm from my own hand
to answer their burning.

We are looking for answers
the abacus can give us.

Suddenly it all adds up:
beads
babies
jellybeans
and birds.
With her trigger finger
Vanessa clicks off
the seventeen days till Christmas.

.